AF484679

WHAT HAPPENED BEFORE, DURING AND AFTER THE BATTLE OF LITTLE BIGHORN?

US History Lessons 4th Grade Children's American History

Speedy Publishing LLC

40 E. Main St. #1156

Newark, DE 19711

www.speedypublishing.com

Copyright 2017

The Battle of the Little Bighorn was a great victory of Native Americans over the United States Army. Why were they fighting? What happened next? Read on and find out!

NATIVE AMERICANS AND AMERICAN COLONISTS WAR

THE FIGHT OVER LAND

The relationship between Native Americans and the people of the United States was often uneasy. The Native Americans resented the newcomers taking their land, and the recent arrivals often felt that the original peoples were less than human and should be removed. It was not a good recipe for peaceful relations!

In 1875, white settlers were moving into the Black Hills area of what is now South Dakota, which Sioux and Cheyenne tribes considered sacred land. Warriors from many tribes came together in Montana under the leadership of Sitting Bull, a great chief and fighter. In 1876, they fought the U.S. Calvalry twice, and won twice.

BLACK HILLS

The U.S. government sent a large detachment of troops to force the tribes back onto their reservations and away from the Black Hills. The troops were in three columns which were supposed to work together. Colonel George Armstrong Custer commanded the Seventh Cavalry, which was part of one of the columns.

SEVENTH CAVALRY

WHO WAS GEORGE ARMSTRONG CUSTER?

"Autie" Custer was a career soldier. He was highly popular with his men and with the public, and less popular with his superior officers. He was headstrong and daring, often taking great risks to achieve unlikely victories.

COLONEL GEORGE ARMSTRONG CUSTER

MILITARY ACADEMY, WEST POINT

Custer graduated from West Point, the military academy, last in his class. He was known more as a trickster and a social fellow rather than the material of a good officer. As an officer in the Union Army in the Civil War, Custer often led his detachments from the front, leading the charge and risking his life over and over.

His troops appreciated this daring, although he was also mocked for being a dandy. Custer was very careful about his clothing and his appearance. He had gold lace on his uniform, a red scarf around his neck, and a broad-brimmed hat—these were the days when officers had a lot of choice about what they wore! He also perfumed his bright-yellow hair with cinnamon oil.

CUSTER

BATTLE OF GETTYSBURG

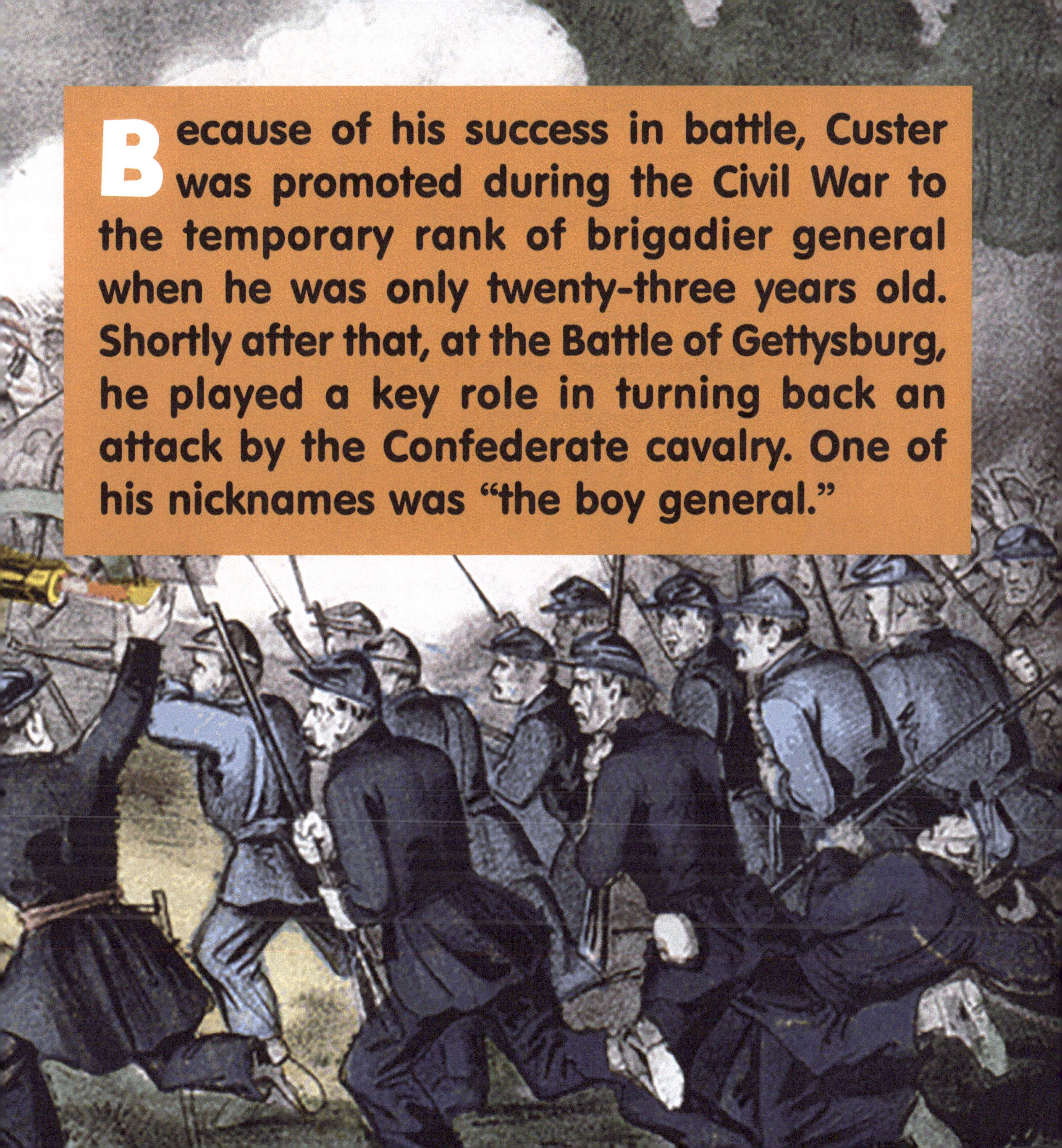
Because of his success in battle, Custer was promoted during the Civil War to the temporary rank of brigadier general when he was only twenty-three years old. Shortly after that, at the Battle of Gettysburg, he played a key role in turning back an attack by the Confederate cavalry. One of his nicknames was "the boy general."

However, Custer was also court-martialed twice for violations of regulations, and his superiors thought his head-strong style would lead him into disaster. Custer rose to the temporary rank of major general, but his permanent rank was captain.

COURT ROOM

BUFFALO BILL CODY

Much of what we think of Custer comes from the many speeches his widow made after his death, and by dramatic performances of the Battle of the Little Bighorn put on by Buffalo Bill Cody in a traveling wild west show. The legend of Custer is perhaps much bigger than the reality will support.

GETTING TO THE LITTLE BIGHORN

The cavalry columns moved slowly forward, seeking to push the tribes north peacefully if possible. However, the government forces were not above burning villages they found.

On June 25, Custer's force located a Sioux village a few miles away, on the edge of the Rosebud River. There were also mounted warriors nearby.

SIOUX VILLAGE

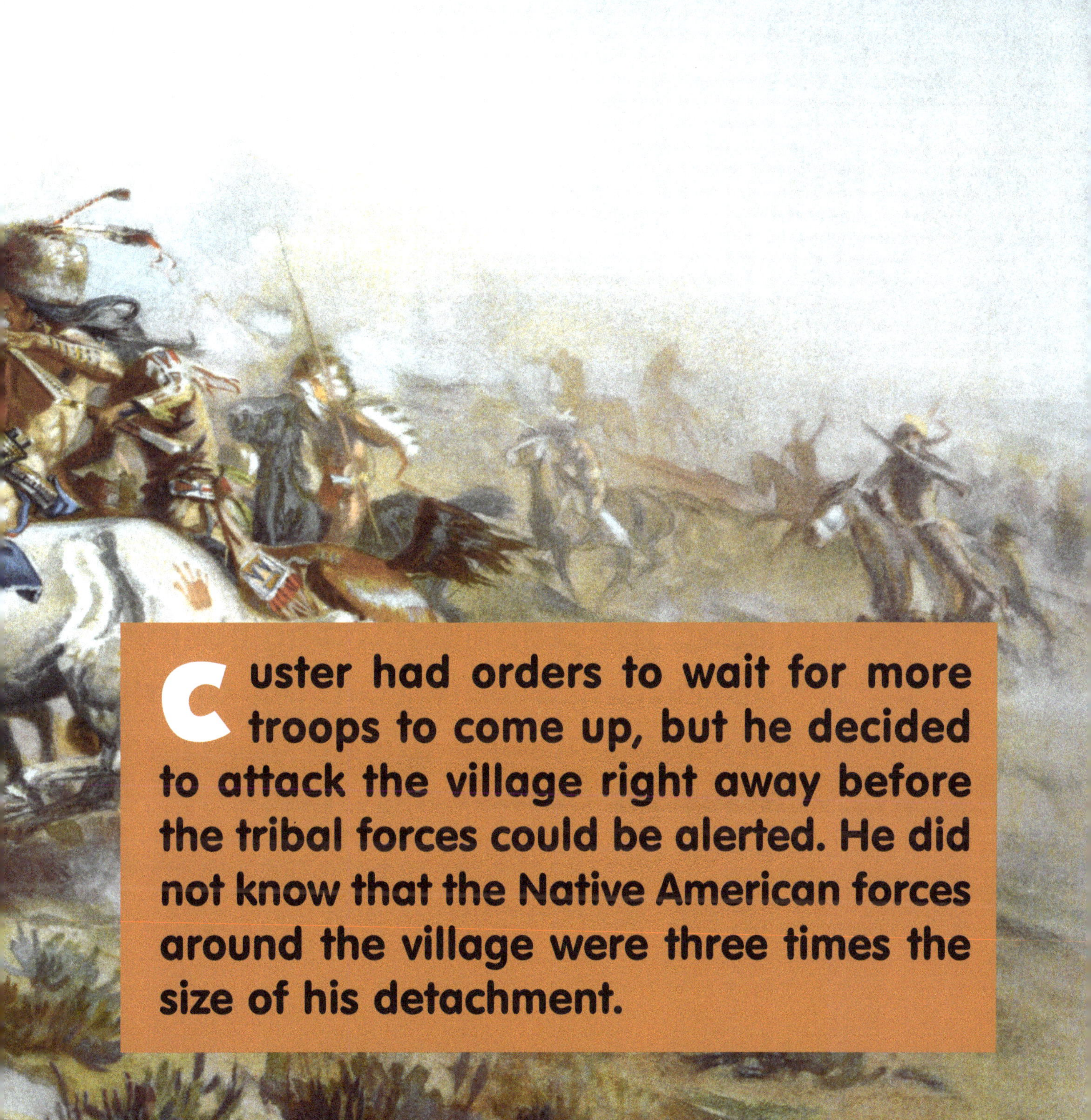

Custer had orders to wait for more troops to come up, but he decided to attack the village right away before the tribal forces could be alerted. He did not know that the Native American forces around the village were three times the size of his detachment.

THE BATTLE

Custer divided his troops into three groups, to attack the village from several sides. The plan went wrong because Custer, not having scouted ahead, did not know the rough ground ahead of his unit would delay his part of the attack.

MAJOR RENO

The group attacking from the north, under Major Reno, was quickly outnumbered and had to retreat to save some of his 175 troops. When Custer's force of over 200 soldiers appeared to the south, Cheyenne and Sioux warriors crossed the Little Bighorn River and attacked Custer from the side.

Custer's force started to retreat toward high ground. Then a Sioux force under Chief Crazy Horse attacked from the south. Custer and his men were outnumbered and surrounded.

CHIEF CRAZY HORSE

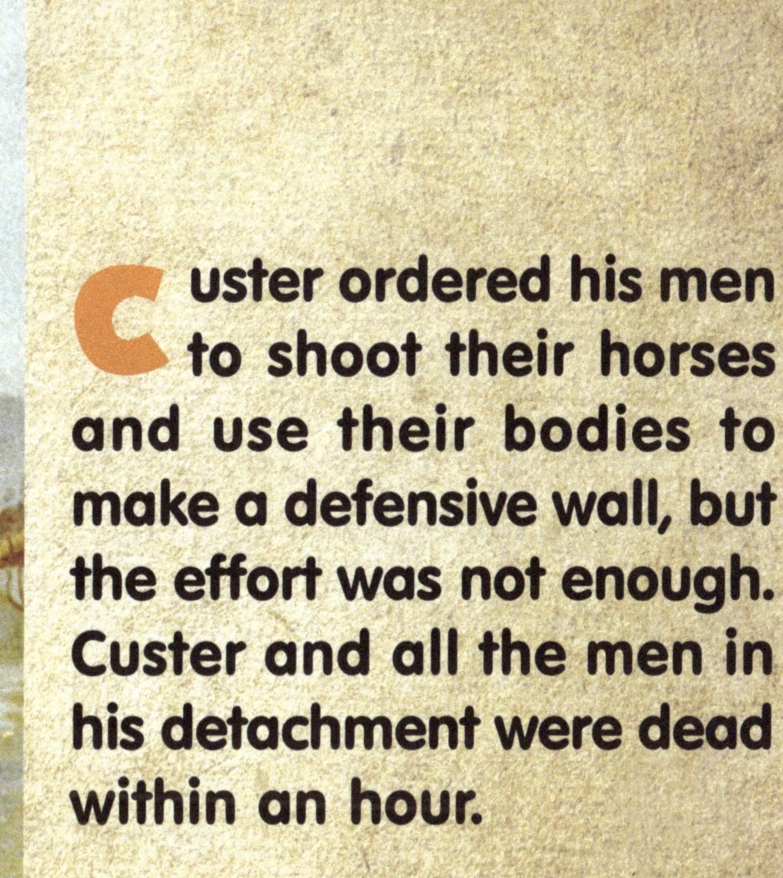

Custer ordered his men to shoot their horses and use their bodies to make a defensive wall, but the effort was not enough. Custer and all the men in his detachment were dead within an hour.

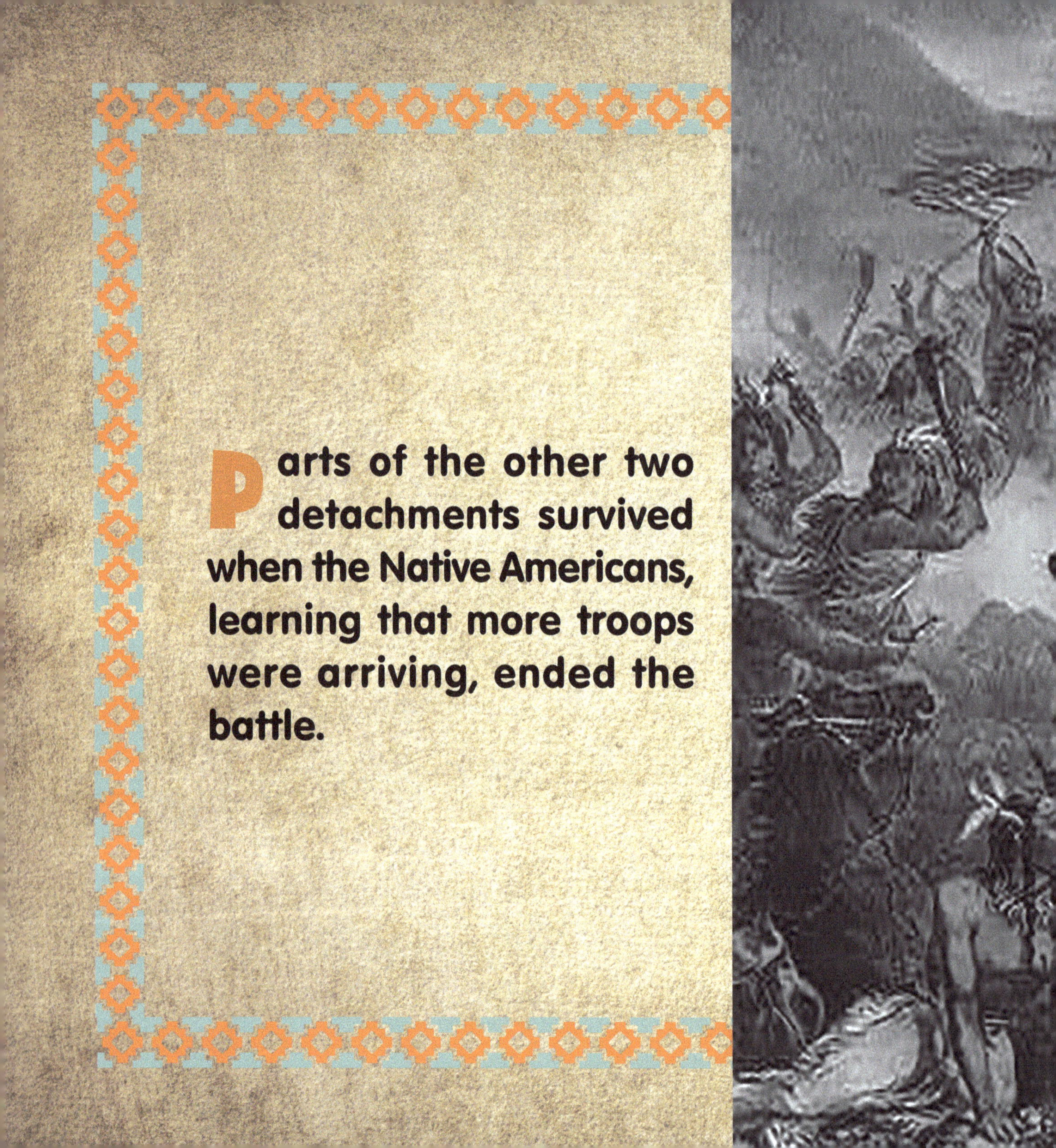

Parts of the other two detachments survived when the Native Americans, learning that more troops were arriving, ended the battle.

CUSTER'S LAST STAND

Custer's defeat and the destruction of his force are remembered as a great U.S. military disaster, far larger than the numbers of those who died might indicate.

SOME FACTS ABOUT THE BATTLE

Here are some interesting things to know about the battle.

- Many of the Native American fighters had better weapons than the cavalry troops did. The soldiers were using single-shot rifles, while over one hundred of the tribal forces had Winchester repeating rifles. As well as being outnumbered, the cavalry troops were seriously out-gunned.

WINCHESTER REPEATING RIFLES

CROW VILLAGE

- Many of the U.S. troops were young men, and possibly not well-trained. Custer, and the army generally, seriously underestimated the abilities of the force they were going to fight.
- The area where the battle took place was traditionally Crow tribal land. The Crow people had allied with the United States and were not part of the battle. The Sioux and Crow tribes often were in conflict. The Sioux, a militant tribe, often stole cattle and horses from Crow villages.

- The Sioux also dominated other tribes, like the Shoshone, the Arikara, and the Blackfeet. In Sioux culture, skill in warfare and raiding were very important.
- The victors at The Little Bighorn took the weapons of the slain soldiers, and many souvenirs. Some found watches, which they kept for a while; but when the ticking stopped the Native Americans did not know how to wind them up or what the watches were for, so they threw them away.

SIX BLACKFEET CHIEFS

COMPASS

- **Other Native Americans found compasses on the soldiers' bodies. They did not understand that the compass needles pointed to the north, instead, they thought somehow the compass was pointing to where other cavalry soldiers were. They thought this was how the white soldiers found each other.**

- Many of the dead men had leather wallets. The Native Americans kept the wallets because they appreciated the quality of the leather and the workmanship. But they threw away the paper money inside the wallets because it had no meaning for them. They did not see that paper money had any value.

LEATHER WALLET

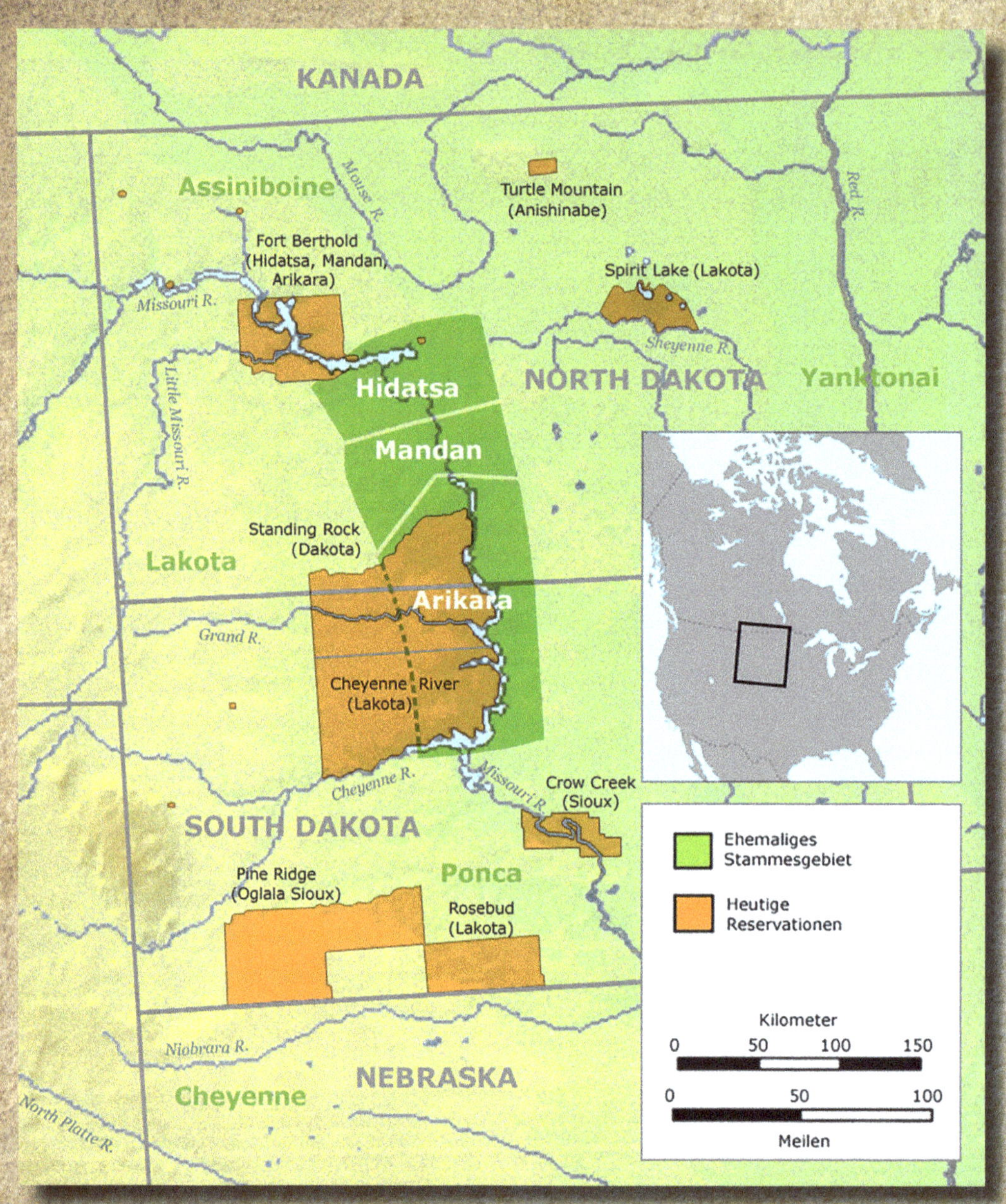

KANADA
Assiniboine
Turtle Mountain
(Anishinabe)
Fort Berthold
(Hidatsa, Mandan,
Arikara)
Spirit Lake (Lakota)
Missouri R.
Mousa R.
Red R.
Hidatsa
NORTH DAKOTA
Yanktonai
Sheyenne R.
Little Missouri R.
Mandan
Standing Rock
(Dakota)
Lakota
Arikara
Grand R.
Cheyenne River
(Lakota)
Cheyenne R.
Missouri R.
Crow Creek
(Sioux)
SOUTH DAKOTA
Pine Ridge
(Oglala Sioux)
Ponca
Rosebud
(Lakota)
Ehemaliges
Stammesgebiet
Heutige
Reservationen
Niobrara R.
NEBRASKA
Cheyenne
North Platte R.
Kilometer
0   50   100   150
0   50   100
Meilen

ARIKARA TERRITORY

One of the scouts for the cavalry was Bobtailed Bull, an Arikara fighter. His horse was named Little Soldier. Bobtailed Bull died at Little Bighorn. Little Soldier found his way back to Arikara territory, over three hundred miles away, after the battle.

- The steamboat "Far West" was supposed to deliver supplies to the cavalry. When Captain Grant Marsh brought the boat to where they were supposed to meet the soldiers, they learned of the disaster and found over fifty wounded soldiers with the troops waiting for them.

STEAMBOAT

FINE GOLD 999.9
NET WT 1000g
GOLD BARS

They took the soldiers on board and steamed south to take the news to the rest of the army. In order to go quickly, they threw overboard a lot of cargo, including gold bars worth over $350,000. That treasure is still lost! The "Far West" was the first to deliver the news of what came to be called Custer's Last Stand.

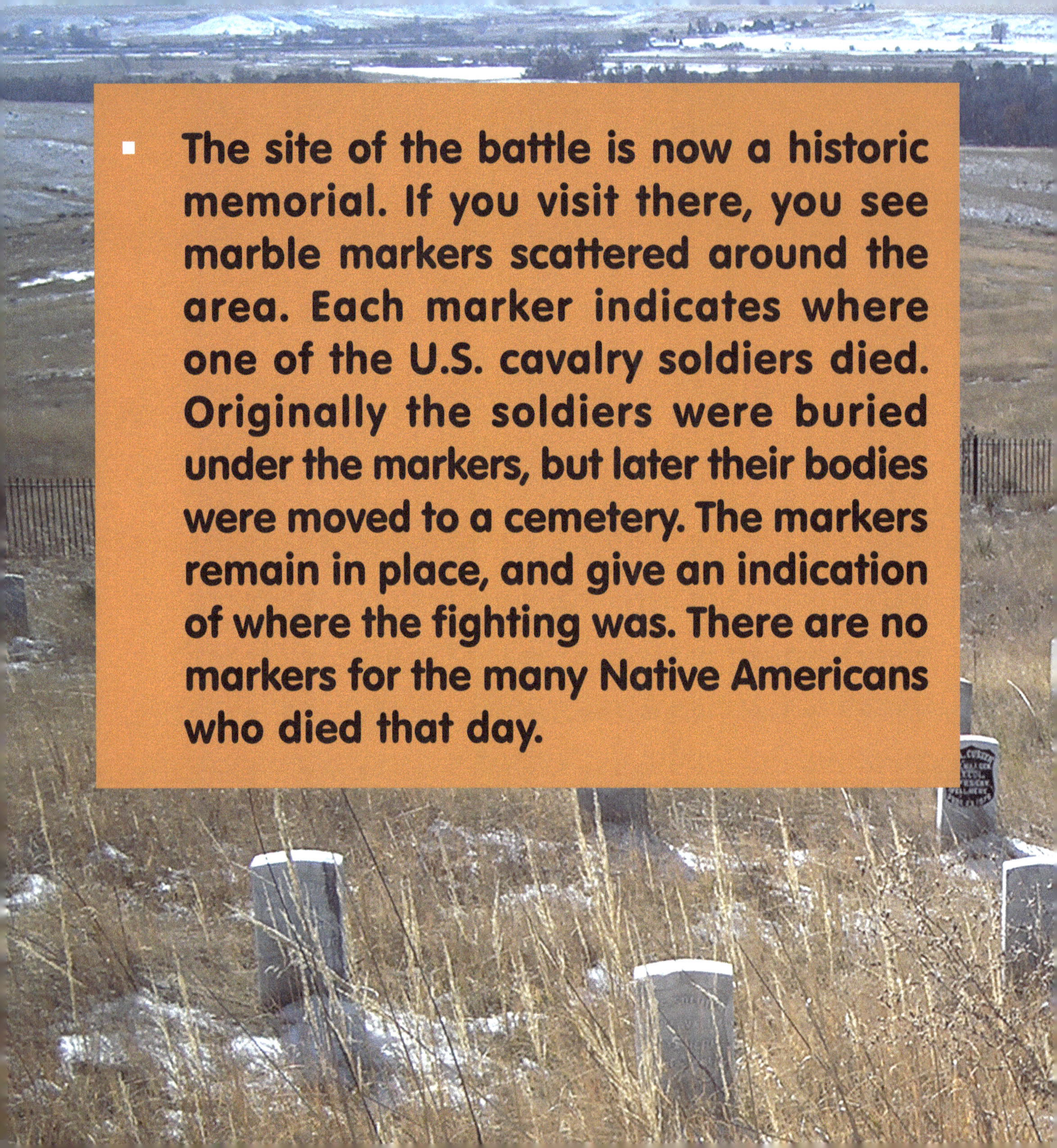

The site of the battle is now a historic memorial. If you visit there, you see marble markers scattered around the area. Each marker indicates where one of the U.S. cavalry soldiers died. Originally the soldiers were buried under the markers, but later their bodies were moved to a cemetery. The markers remain in place, and give an indication of where the fighting was. There are no markers for the many Native Americans who died that day.

LITTLE BIGHORN BATTLEFIELD NATIONAL MONUMENT

THOMAS CUSTER

- **Along with George Armstrong Custer, four other members of his family died at the battle. They were his brother-in-law, James Calhoun; his younger brothers Boston and Tom; and his nephew, Henry Reed, who was only eighteen.**
- **Tom Custer was a veteran of the Civil War, and had received the Congressional Medal of Honor for gallantry—twice!**

WHAT HAPPENED AFTER

The Little Bighorn victory was the high point of the resistance to United State expansion into Native American territory. However, the alliance of tribes came apart very soon. The federal government changed the boundaries of reservation lands so that the Black Hills were not included and therefore were available for white settlers. A year after Custer's death, the tribe offering the most resistance, the Sioux, were defeated and confined to a reservation.

NATIVE INDIAN RESERVATION, NEW MEXICO

NATIVE AMERICANS AND THEIR LAND

The Native American experience goes back tens of thousands of years, as hundreds of tribes and millions of people occupied what is now the United States. Learn more about the first inhabitants of the country in Little Professor books like Getting to Know the Great Native American Tribes, King Philip's War, and The World is Full of Spirits.

Visit
BABY PROFESSOR
EDUCATION KIDS
www.BabyProfessorBooks.com
to download Free Baby Professor eBooks and view
our catalog of new and exciting Children's Books